PMF
BA

JOSEPH WRIGHT OF DERBY

Frontispiece   *Self-portrait* c 1767–68
Charles Rogers–Coltman   Cat 167

Joseph Wright of Derby

Painter of Light

Volume Two
Plates

Benedict Nicolson

STUDIES IN
BRITISH ART

The Paul Mellon Foundation for British Art
London Routledge and Kegan Paul Limited
New Haven Yale University Press

First published in Great Britain 1968
by The Paul Mellon Foundation for British Art, 38 Bury Street,
London, S.W. 1 in association with Routledge & Kegan Paul Ltd.,
Broadway House, Carter Lane, London, E.C. 4

Barnard
ND
497
. W8
N 5

V. 2

ISBN 0-300-0-1489-9
Library of Congress catalogue card no. 68–28393
Printed in the Netherlands by Joh. Enschedé en Zonen, Haarlem
Bound in the Netherlands by N.V. Boekbinderij P. M. Jansen
Designed by Paul Sharp in the offices of
The Paul Mellon Foundation for British Art

List of Subjects

References are to the Catalogue (Volume 1, pp 171–272) and to the Plates, the latter in bold type. Reference is only made to Figures (Volume 1) when these provide significant details

List of Collections and Owners

The numbers refer to the catalogue entries in Volume 1 and the plate numbers in Volume 2. Plate numbers are shown in bold type.
Only works included in the catalogue are listed.

The Plates

The plates are arranged in an approximately chronological order. The choice of works for illustration in colour has been largely determined by their suitability for reproduction on a small scale. In the captions all question marks refer to dates.

The following plates have had to be made from old photographs and are therefore of inferior quality: plates 47, 189, 273, 300.

Plate 1   Copy of an engraving c 1748–50
Pencil and sepia wash 6 x 9⅞ in / 15.2 x 25 cm
Derby Museum and Art Gallery

Plate 2　*Head of John Rotherham* 1751
Black chalk with white heightening
15¼ x 11⅜ in / 38.7 x 28.9 cm
Derby Museum and Art Gallery

Plate 4　*Nathaniel Curzon, 2nd Baron
Scarsdale* c 1755–56
19 x 15 in / 48.2 x 38.1 cm
Viscount Scarsdale　Cat 48

Plate 3　*Head of Judith, from Piazzetta's Judith and
Holofernes* 1751
Black chalk with white heightening
15¼ x 11⅜ in / 38.7 x 28.9 cm
Michael and Elizabeth Ayrton

Plate 5　*Lady Caroline Curzon* c 1755–56
18 x 16⅛ in / 45.7 x 41.3 cm
Captain P. J. B. Drury-Lowe　Cat 49

Plate 6   *Self-portrait* c 1758
30 x 25 in / 76.2 x 63.5 cm
Miss D. M. R. Cade   Cat 164

Plate 7   *Self-portrait* c 1758
Pencil 4⅜ x 3¾ in / 11.1 x 9.5 cm
Fitzwilliam Museum, Cambridge

Plate 8   *Portrait of a Boy* 1758
22 x 18 in / 55.9 x 45.7 cm   Mrs Karl F. Milde   Cat 158

Plate 9   *Richard Staunton Wilmot* c 1760
20 x 16 in / 50.8 x 40.6 cm
Peter Wilmot-Sitwell   Cat 142

Plate 10   *Harvey Wilmot* c 1760
20 x 16 in / 50.8 x 40.6 cm
Peter Wilmot-Sitwell   Cat 147

Plate 11   *Dorothy Wilmot* c 1760
20 x 16 in / 50.8 x 40.6 cm
Peter Wilmot-Sitwell   Cat 143

Plate 12   *Edward Sacheverell Wilmot* c 1760
20 x 16 in / 50.8 x 40.6 cm
Peter Wilmot-Sitwell   Cat 144

Plate 13   *Simon Wilmot* c 1760
20 x 16 in / 50.8 x 40.6 cm
Peter Wilmot-Sitwell   Cat 146

Plate 15   *Robert Wilmot* c 1760
20 x 16 in / 50.8 x 40.6 cm
Peter Wilmot-Sitwell   Cat 145

Plate 14   *Miss Elizabeth Lygon* c 1760
30 x 25 in / 76.2 x 63.5 cm
Private Collection U.K.   Cat 103

Plate 16   *'Dorothy Anne, Wife of Col Charles
Heathcote'* c 1760
? 30 x 25 in / 76.2 x 63.5 cm
Untraced   Cat 80

Plate 17   *Reginald Lygon* c 1760
30 x 25 in / 76.2 x 63.5 cm
Private collection U.K.   Cat 101

Plate 18   *Mrs Susannah Lygon* c 1760
30 x 25 in / 76.2 x 63.5 cm
Private collection U.K.   Cat 102

Plate 19   *William Kirke* 1759–60
30 x 25 in / 76.2 x 63.5 cm
Rear Admiral David Kirke   Cat 98

Plate 20   *Nicholas Hutchinson* 1760
30 x 25 in / 76.2 x 63.5 cm
Jeremy Hutchinson Q. C.   Cat 96

Plate 21   *William Brooke* 1760
50 x 40 in / 127 x 101.6 cm
R. D. Plant   Cat 25

Plate 22   *Mrs Ann Carver* 1760
50 x 40 in / 127 x 101.6 cm
Mr and Mrs Ronald Tree   Cat 28

Plate 23   *William Pigot* 1760
50 x 40 in / 127 x 101.6 cm
R. D. Plant   Cat 120

Plate 24   *Mrs William Pigot* 1760
50 x 40 in / 127 x 101.6 cm
R. D. Plant   Cat 121

Plate 25   *'Rebecca' Cracroft* 1760
50 x 40 in / 127 x 101.6 cm
Private collection U.K.   Cat 45

Plate 26 *Miss Ann Carver* 1760
50 x 40 in / 127 x 101.6 cm
Mr and Mrs Ronald Tree Cat 29

Plate 27   *Rev John C. Carver of Morthen* 1760
50 x 40 in / 127 x 101.6 cm
Formerly Athorpe Collection   Cat 31

Plate 28   *Miss Elizabeth Carver* 1760
50 x 40 in / 127 x 101.6 cm
Formerly Athorpe Collection   Cat 30

Plate 29 *Young Girl* c 1760
16 x 13 in / 40.6 x 33 cm
Leeds City Art Gallery and Temple
Newsam House   Cat 160

Plate 30   *Thomas Bennett* c 1760
30 x 25 in / 76.2 x 63.5 cm
Derby Museum and Art Gallery   Cat 16

Plate 31   'Miss Catton' or 'Miss Cotton' c 1760
50 x 40 in / 127 x 101.6 cm
City Art Museum of Saint Louis   Cat 34

Plate 32   Female Portrait c 1760
30 x 25 in / 76.2 x 63.5 cm
Dr and Mrs Merlin L. Trumbull   Cat 159

Plate 33 *Edward Becher Leacroft of Wirksworth* c 1762–63
50 x 40 in / 127 x 101.6 cm
Major Peter Miller Mundy Cat 99

Plate 34   *Francis Noel Clarke Mundy of Markeaton* c 1762–63
50 x 40 in / 127 x 101.6 cm
Major Peter Miller Mundy   Cat 110

Plate 35   *Harry Peckham* c 1762–63
50 x 40 in / 127 x 101.6 cm
Major Peter Miller Mundy   Cat 117

Plate 36   *Launcelot Rolliston* c 1762–63
50 x 40 in / 127 x 101.6 cm
Major Peter Miller Mundy   Cat 127

Plate 37   *Nicholas Heath* c 1762–63
50 x 40 in / 127 x 101.6 cm
Major Peter Miller Mundy   Cat 77

Plate 38   *Francis Burdett of Foremark* c 1762–63
50 x 40 in / 127 x 101.6 cm
Major Peter Miller Mundy   Cat 27

Plate 39   *Thomas Borrow* c 1762–63
50 x 40 in / 127 x 101.6 cm
Derby Museum and Art Gallery   Cat 21

Plate 40 *Mrs Wilmot* c 1762–63
50 x 40 in / 127 x 101.6 cm
Sir Robert Wilmot Bt   Cat 148

Plate 41   *Mrs William Chase* c 1761–63
30 x 25 in / 76.2 x 63.5 cm
Yale University Art Gallery; gift of Junius S. and Henry
S. Morgan   Cat 36

Plate 42   *Young Man* c 1762–64
30 x 25 in / 76.2 x 63.5 cm
Private collection U.K.   Cat 157

Plate 43   '*Mr Mundy*' c 1762–64
30 x 25 in / 76.2 x 63.5 cm
Sir Gilbert Inglefield   Cat 113

Plate 44   '*Mrs Mundy*' c 1762–63
30 x 25 in / 76.2 x 63.5 cm
Sir Gilbert Inglefield   Cat 112

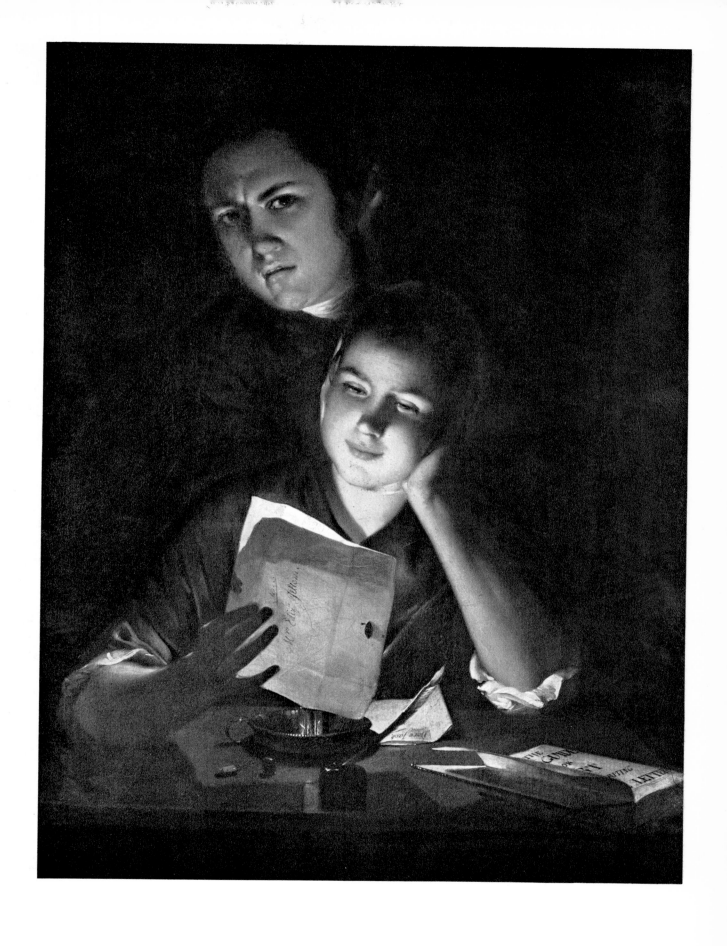

Plate 45   *A Girl reading a Letter by candlelight, with a
Young Man looking over her shoulder* c 1762–63
35 x 27½ in / 88.9 x 69.8 cm
Lt Col R. S. Nelthorpe   Cat 207

Plate 46 'Hon. Mrs Boyle' c 1761–63
30 x 25 in / 76.2 x 63.5 cm
The Mackelvie Collection, Auckland City Art Gallery
Cat 23

Plate 47   Female Portrait c 1761–63
Untraced   Cat 162

26

Plate 48 *Frances Warren* c 1762–64
50 x 40 in / 127 x 101.6 cm
Mrs Gerard Sweetman Cat 138

Plate 49 *Hon Richard Fitzwilliam, later
7th Viscount Fitzwilliam of Merrion* 1764
30 x 25 in / 76.2 x 63.5 cm
Fitzwilliam Museum, Cambridge
Cat 60

Plate 50   *Mr and Mrs William Chase* c 1762–3
54½ x 75 in / 138.4 x 190.5 cm
Lord Butler   Cat 37

Plate 51   *James Shuttleworth, his Wife and Daughter* 1764
56 x 72 in / 142.2 x 182.9 cm
Lord Shuttleworth   Cat 129

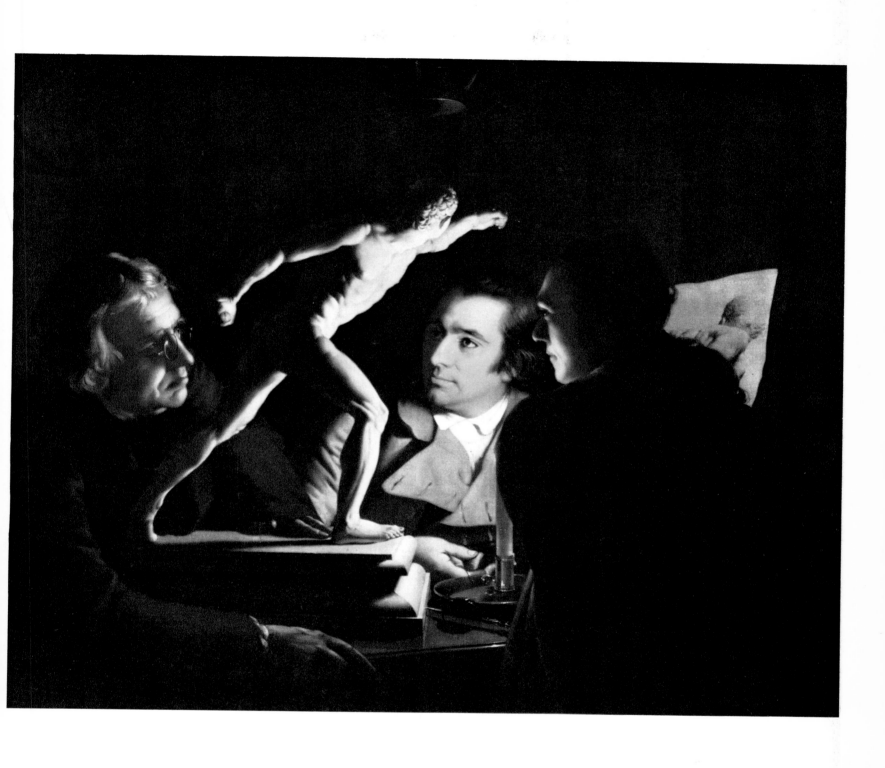

Plate 52   *Three Persons viewing the Gladiator by Candlelight* c 1764–65
40 x 48 in / 101.6 x 121.9 cm
Private collection, U.K.   Cat 188

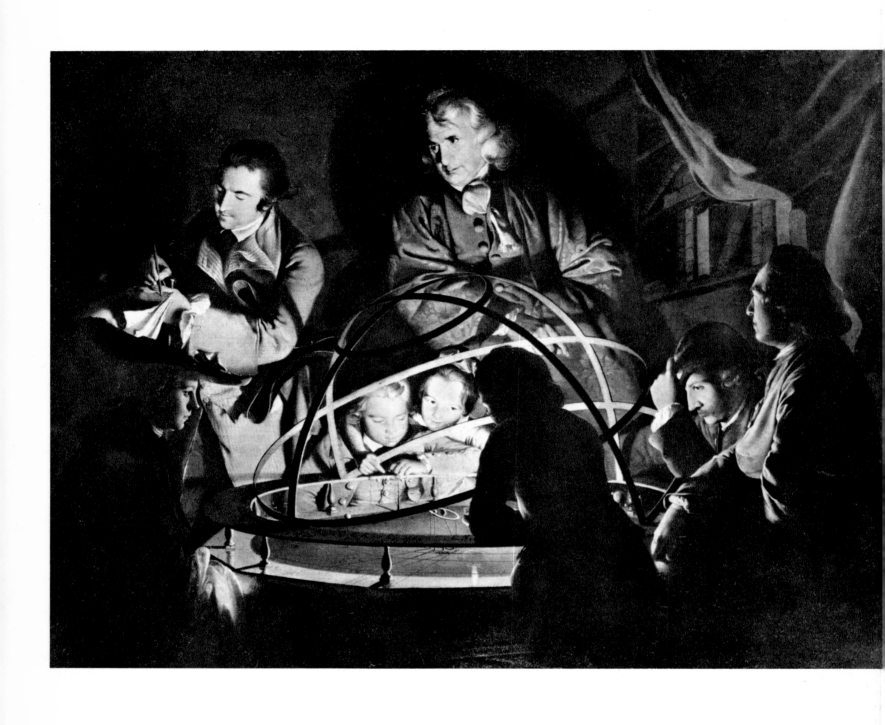

Plate 53   *A Philosopher giving a Lecture on the Orrery* c 1768
Monochrome study for engraving 17¾ x 23 in / 45 x 58.4 cm
Mr and Mrs Paul Mellon   Cat 191

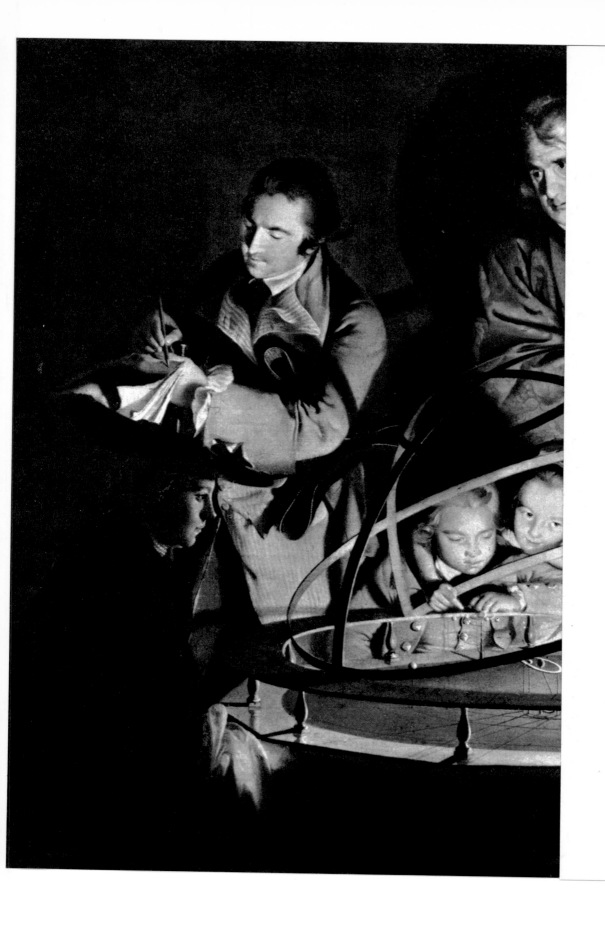

Plate 54   *A Philosopher giving a lecture on the Orrery* c 1764–66
58 x 80 in / 147.3 x 203.2 cm
Derby Museum and Art Gallery   Cat 190

Plate 55 *Mrs Gwillym of Atherton* 1766
50 x 40 in / 127 x 101.6 cm
City Art Museum of Saint Louis   Cat 69

Plate 56   *Robert Vernon Atherton Gwillym* 1766
50 x 40 in / 127 x 101.6 cm
City Art Museum of Saint Louis   Cat 68

Plate 57 *Bradshaw Children* c 1766–68
63½ x 54 in / 161.3 x 137.2 cm
Peter Wilmot-Sitwell Cat 24

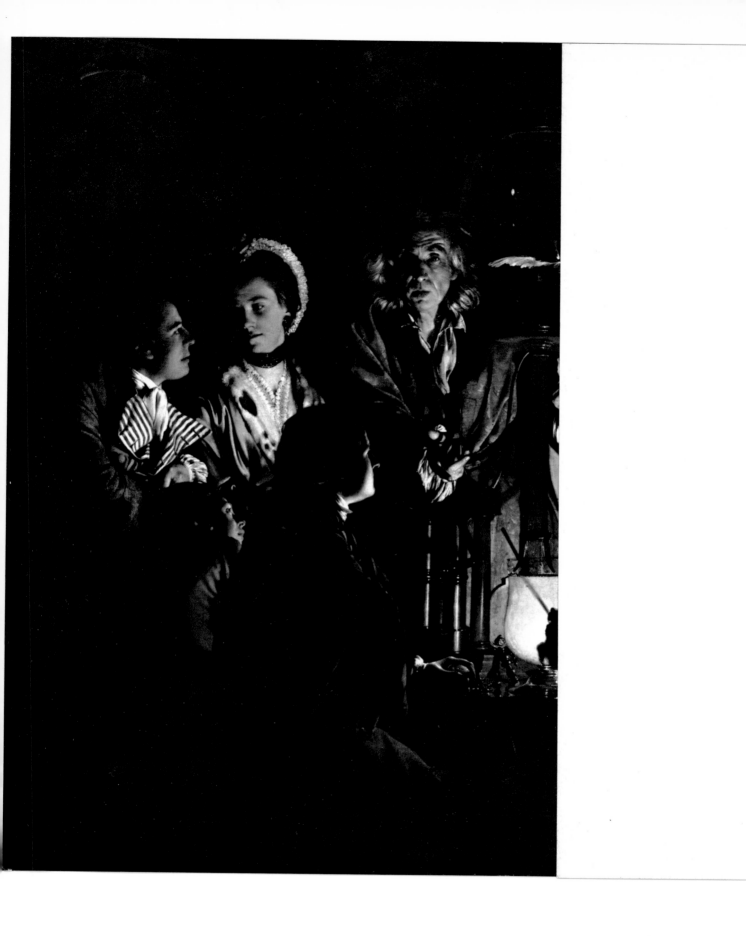

Plate 58   *An Experiment on a Bird in the Air Pump* c 1767–68
72 x 96 in / 182.9 x 243.8 cm
Tate Gallery   Cat 192

Plate 59 *Study for An Experiment on a Bird in the Air Pump*
(on reverse of *Self portrait—Frontispiece*) c 1767
24½ x 30 in / 62.2 x 76.2 cm
Charles Rogers-Coltman   Cat 193

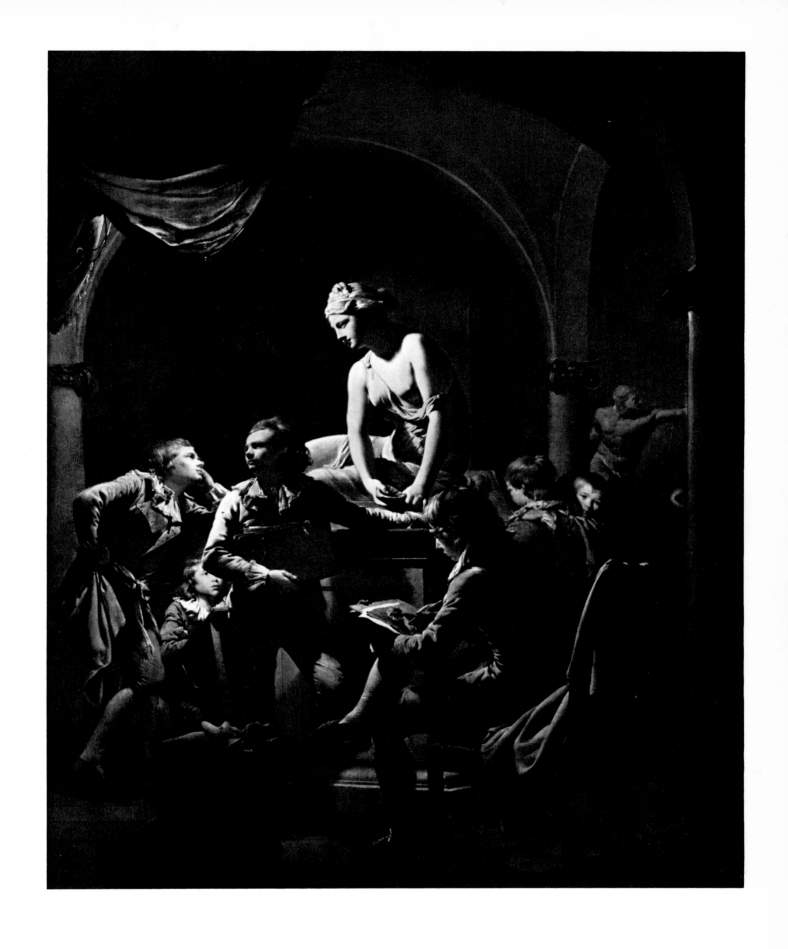

Plate 60   *An Academy by Lamplight* c 1768–69
50 x 39⅞ in / 127 x 101.2 cm
Mr and Mrs Paul Mellon
on loan to the Tate Gallery   Cat 189

Plate 61   *Fleetwood Hesketh* 1769
50 x 40 in / 127 x 101.6 cm
Trustees of the Hesketh Settled Estate   Cat 81

38

Plate 62   *Frances Hesketh* 1769
50 x 40 in / 127 x 101.6 cm
Trustees of the Hesketh Settled Estate   Cat 82

39

Plate 63   *Mrs Sarah Clayton* c 1769
50 x 40 in / 127 x 101.6 cm
Fitchburg Art Museum, Mass
gift of Miss Louise I. Doyle   Cat 39

Plate 64   *Mrs John Ashton* 1769
50 x 40 in / 127 x 101.6 cm
Fitzwilliam Museum, Cambridge   Cat 6

Plate 65 *Anna Ashton (Mrs Thomas Case)* 1769
c 50 x 40 in / 127 x 101.6 cm
Captain Everard Radcliffe, M. C.   Cat 8

Plate 66   *Elizabeth Ashton (Mrs John Bostock)* 1769
c 50 x 40 in / 127 x 101.6 cm
David Ashton-Bostock   Cat 7

Plate 67   *Mrs Nicholas Ashton* 1769
50 x 40 in / 127 x 101.6 cm
David Ashton-Bostock   Cat 9

Plate 68   Copy of destroyed work by Wright *John Ashton* 1769
50 x 40 in / 127 x 101.6 cm
David Ashton-Bostock   Cat 10

Plate 69   *Self-portrait ?* 1768
Charcoal 17 x 11⅝ in / 43.2 x 29.5 cm
Mr and Mrs Paul Mellon   Cat 166

Plate 71   *Self-portrait* c 1765–68
Charcoal on bluish paper with white
heightening
16¾ x 11⅝ in / 42.5 x 29.5 cm
James Ricau   Cat 165

Plate 70   *Self-portrait* c 1767–70
Charcoal 21 x 14½ in / 53.3 x 36.8 cm
Derby Museum and Art Gallery   Cat 168

Plate 72   *Thomas Staniforth* 1769
$36\frac{1}{4}$ x 30 in / 92.1 x 76.2 cm
Tate Gallery   Cat 132

Plate 73   *Two Girls and a Negro Servant* c 1769–70
50 x 40 in / 127 x 101.6 cm
Heirs of Oliver Vernon Watney   Cat 163

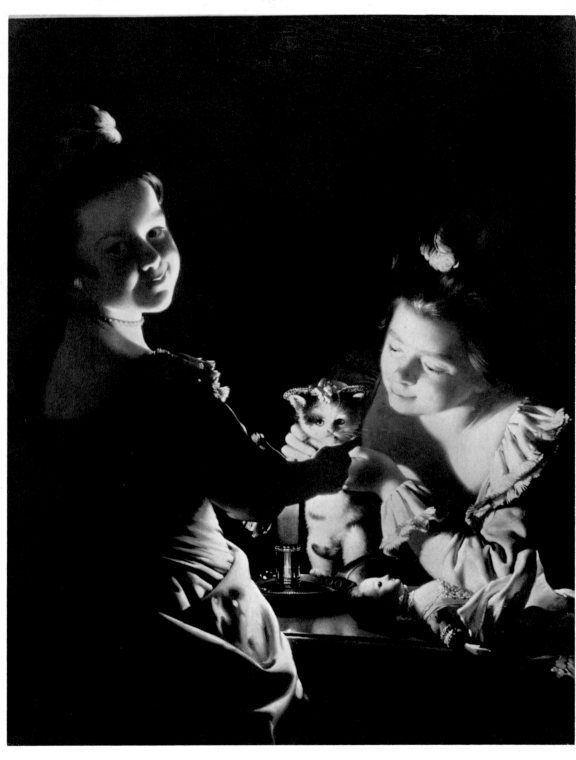

Plate 74   Copy of a lost Wright *Two Boys with a Bladder* original c 1769–70
36 x 28 in / 91.4 x 71.1 cm
Henry E. Huntington Library and Art Gallery   Cat 208

Plate 75   *Two Girls decorating a kitten by candlelight* c 1768–70
35¾ x 28½ in / 90.8 x 72.4 cm
Mrs C. Margaret Riley   Cat 212

Plate 76   *Two Boys fighting over a Bladder* c 1767–70
36 x 28 in / 91.4 x 71.1 cm
Charles Rogers–Coltman   Cat 206

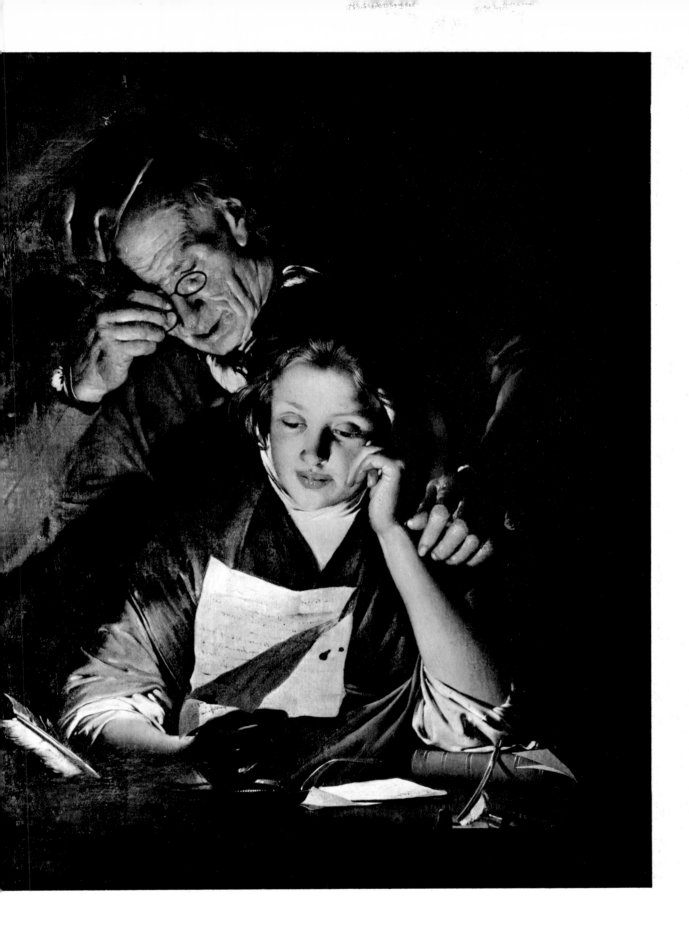

Plate 77   *A Girl reading a letter with an old man reading over her
shoulder* c 1767–70
36 x 28 in / 94.4 x 71.1 cm
Charles Rogers–Coltman   Cat 205

Plate 78 *Erasmus Darwin* 1770
30 x 25 in / 76.2 x 63.5 cm
G. P. Darwin; on loan to Darwin College, Cambridge   Cat 50

Plate 79   *Sarah Carver and her daughter Sarah* c 1769–70
50 x 40 in / 127 x 101.6 cm
Derby Museum and Art Gallery   Cat 32

Plate 80 *Thomas Day* 1770
50 x 40 in / 127 x 101.6 cm
The Lord Belper   Cat 58

Plate 81 '*Mrs Catherine Swindell*' c 1769–71
28 x 22 in / 71.1 x 55.9 cm
Leicester Museum and Art Gallery   Cat 134

Plate 82   *Young Artist* c 1770
c 50 x 40 in / 127 x 101.6 cm
Private Collection U.K.   Cat 156

Plate 83 *Captain Henry Bathurst* c 1770–71
30 x 25 in / 76.2 x 63.5 cm
Lady Hervey-Bathurst   Cat 14

Plate 84 *Mrs Henry Bathurst* c 1770–71
30 x 25 in / 76.2 x 63.5 cm
Lady Hervey-Bathurst   Cat 15

Plate 85   *Captain Richard French* c 1771–72
30 x 25 in / 76.2 x 63.5 cm
L. B. Sanderson   Cat 64

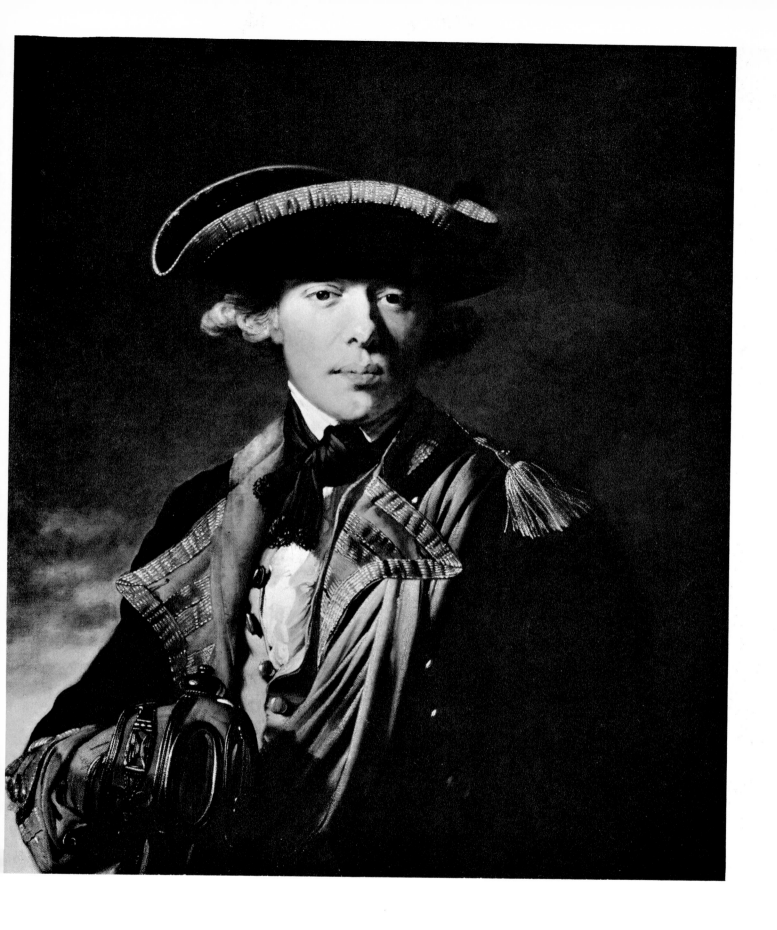

Plate 86   *Sir George Cooke, Bart* c 1770–71
30 x 25 in / 76.2 x 63.5 cm
Nelson Gallery–Atkins Museum (Nelson Fund),
Kansas City   Cat 44

Plate 87   *Colonel Edward Sacheverell Pole* 1772
36 x 30 in / 91.4 x 76.2 cm
Major J. W. Chandos-Pole   Cat 122

Plate 88   *Elizabeth, wife of Edward Sacheverell Pole, and her son Sacheverell* 1771
91¾ x 68¼ in / 233 x 173.3 cm
Major J. W. Chandos-Pole   Cat 123

Plate 89   *Study for portrait of Mrs Sacheverell Pole and her son* c 1771
Gouache on paper with some brown wash
18¼ x 11¾ in / 45.3 x 29.8 cm
Derby Museum and Art Gallery

Plate 90   'Richard, Earl Howe' early '70's
50 x 40 in / 127 x 101.6 cm
National Gallery of Art, Washington D.C.   Cat 91

Plate 91   *Mr and Mrs Thomas Coltman* c 1771–72
50 x 40 in / 127 x 101.6 cm
Charles Rogers–Coltman   Cat 41

Plate 92   *Girl reading a letter* 1772
Major J. W. Chandos-Pole   Cat 201

Plate 93   *Boy and Girl blowing bubbles* 1772
Major J. W. Chandos-Pole   Cat 202

Plate 94   *Old Woman reading a letter in company of a young girl*
1772
Major J. W. Chandos-Pole   Cat 203

Plate 95   *Two Boys blowing on a Bladder* 1772
Major J. W. Chandos-Pole   Cat 204

Plate 96   *Glass-blowing Factory* c 1770–72
Brown ink and grey wash, sight size $14\frac{3}{8}$ x $20\frac{7}{8}$ in / 36.5 x 53 cm
Derby Museum and Art Gallery

Plate 97   *Glass-blowing Factory* c 1770–72
Pen and wash $14\frac{1}{4}$ x $20\frac{1}{2}$ in / 36 x 52 cm
Derby Museum and Art Gallery

Plate 98   *Study of open hearth with fire ?* c 1770–72
Sepia wash with touches of brown ink
Sight size 11 x 12 in / 27.9 x 30.4 cm
Derby Museum and Art Gallery

Plate 99   *Study for an Iron Forge* 1772
Pen and wash heightened with white 12⅝ x 20½ in / 31.1 x 50.5 cm
Derby Museum and Art Gallery

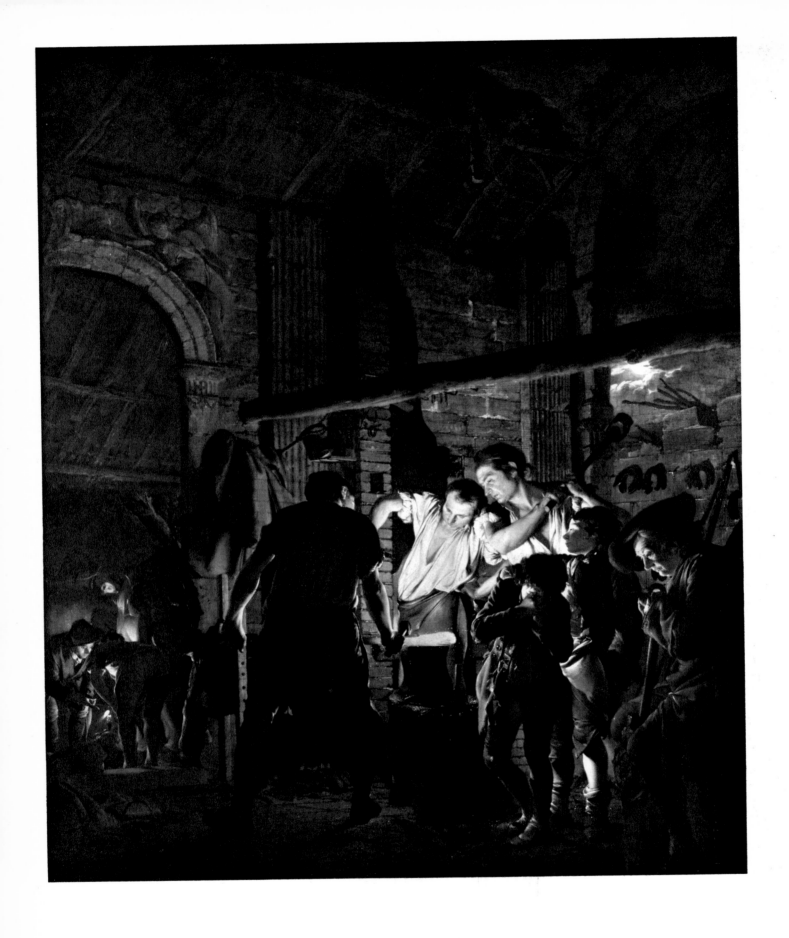

Plate 100　*The Blacksmith's Shop* 1771
50½ x 41 in / 128.2 x 104.1 cm
Mr and Mrs Paul Mellon　Cat 199

Plate 101   *The Blacksmith's Shop* 1771
49½ x 39 in / 125.7 x 99 cm
Private Collection U.K.   Cat 200

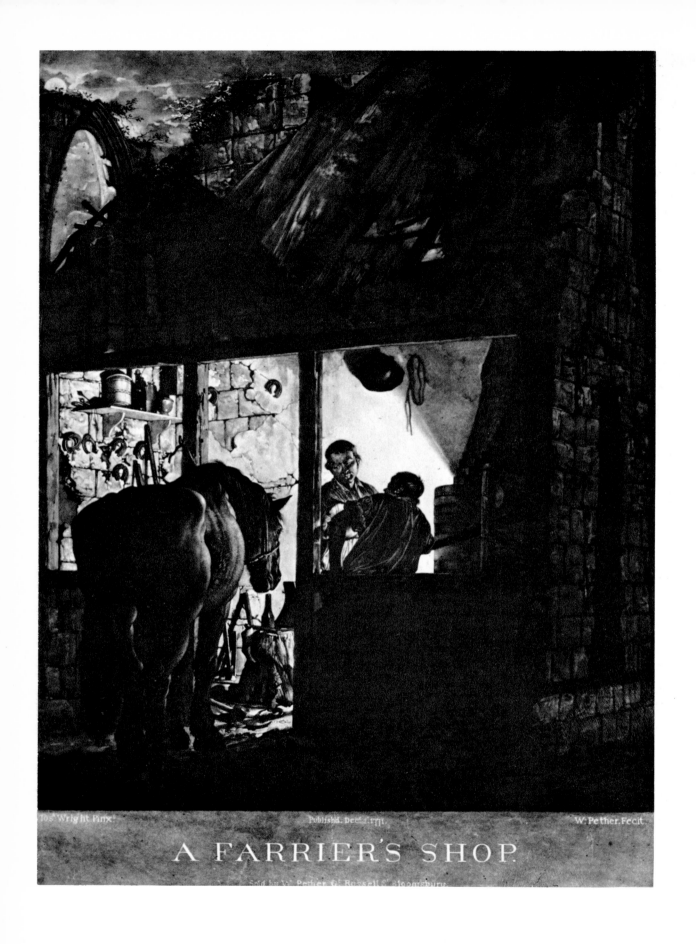

Plate 102 Engraving by W. Pether after Wright
A Farrier's Shop 1771

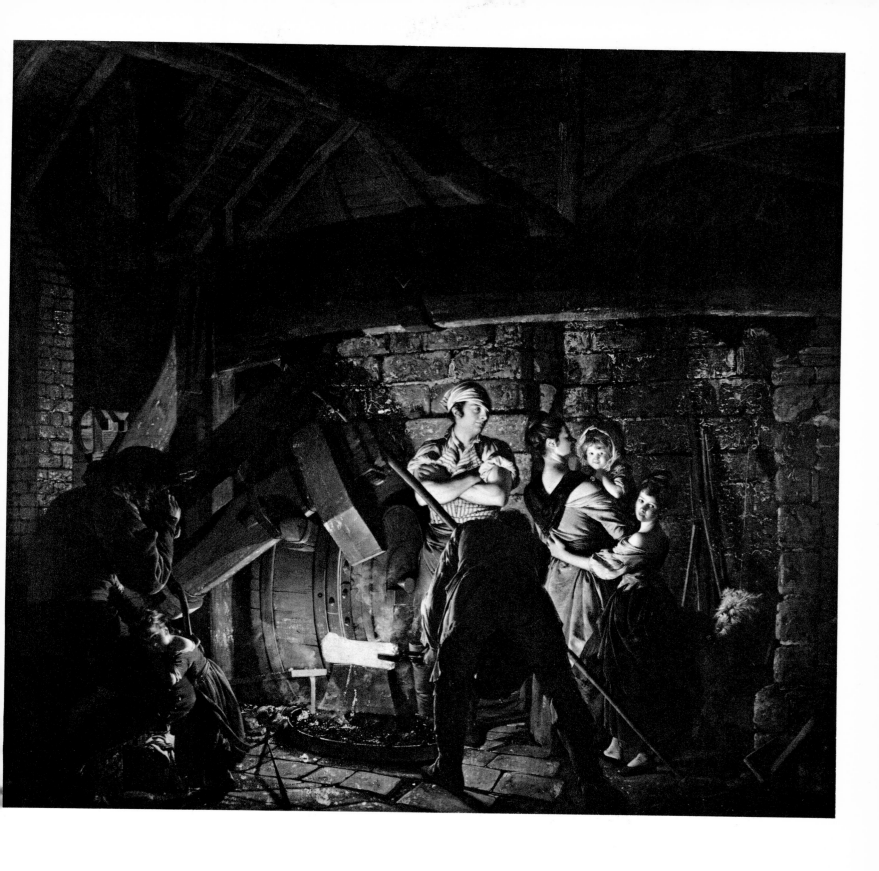

Plate 103   *An Iron Forge* 1772
48 x 52 in / 121.9 x 132.1 cm
Admiral of the Fleet The Earl Mountbatten of Burma   Cat 197

Plate 104 *An Iron Forge viewed from without* 1773
41 x 55 in / 104.1 x 139.7 cm
Hermitage Museum, Leningrad   Cat 198

Plate 105   *Hermit studying Anatomy* c 1771–73
50½ x 40½ in / 128.2 x 102.9 cm
Derby Museum and Art Gallery   Cat 196

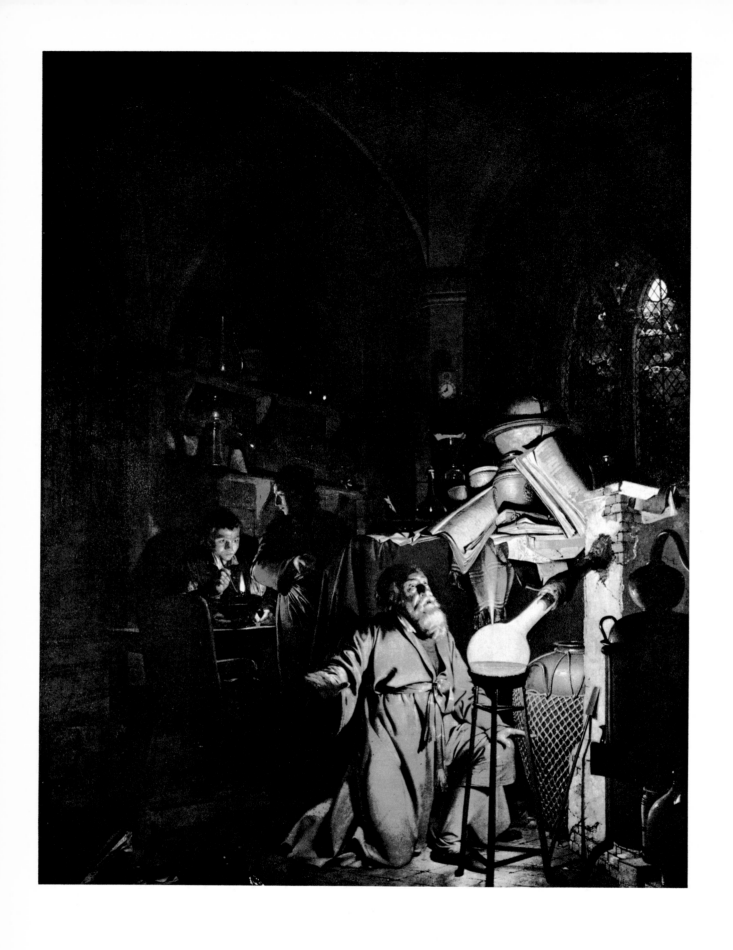

Plate 106 *The Alchemist in search of the Philosopher's Stone
discovers Phosphorus* 1771/1795
50 x 40 in / 127 x 101.6 cm
Derby Museum and Art Gallery   Cat 195

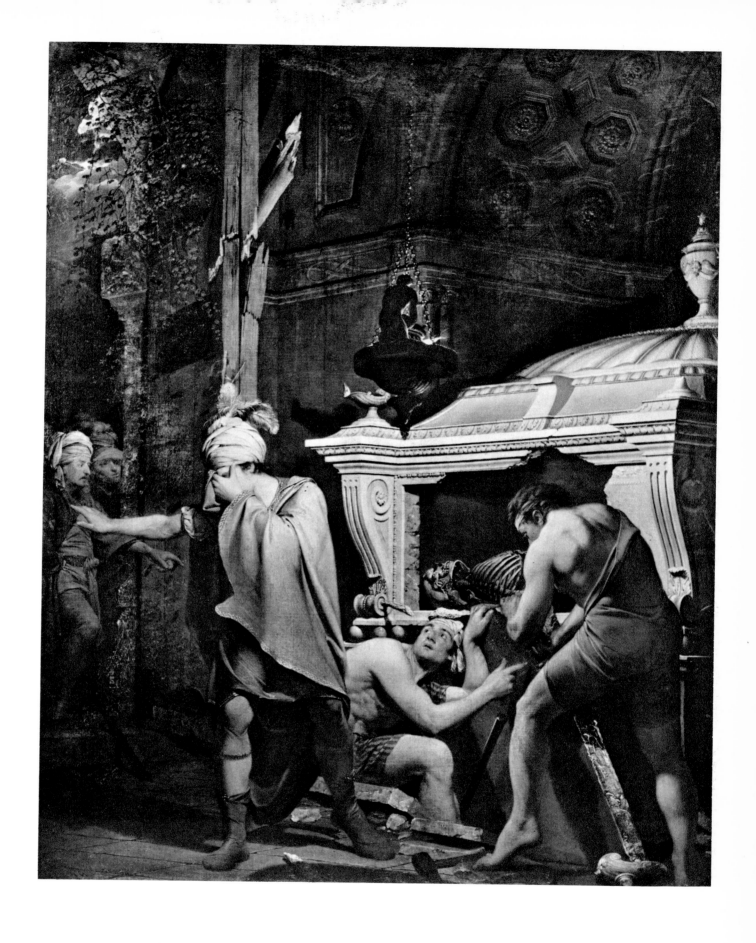

Plate 107   *Miravan opening the Tomb of his Ancestors* 1772
50 x 40 in / 127 x 101.6 cm
Derby Museum and Art Gallery   Cat 222

Plate 108 Study for the *Captive King* c 1772–73
Pen and wash 13¼ x 15⅝ in / 33.6 x 39.6 cm
Derby Museum and Art Gallery

Plate 109 *Study for the Captive King* 1772
Pen and wash
Untraced

Plate 110   *The Captive King* c 1772
12 x 14¼ in / 30.4 x 36.2 cm
Basil Taylor   Cat 215

Plate 111   Sketch for the *Captive King*
from a letter to P. P. Burdett
Pen and ink
Herman W. Liebert

Plate 112   *Rocks with Waterfall* c 1771–72
Size unknown
Major J. W. Chandos-Pole   Cat 328

Plate 113   *The Earthstopper on the Banks of the Derwent* 1773
38 x 47½ in / 96.5 x 120.6 cm
Derby Museum and Art Gallery   Cat 242

Plate 114 'Captain' Robert Shore Milnes c 1771–72
50 x 40 in / 127 x 101.6 cm
Mrs Lawrence Copley Thaw   Cat 107

Plate 115   Colonel Charles Heathcote
c 1771–72
50 x 40 in / 127 x 101.6 cm
Untraced   Cat 79

Plate 116   *British Gun-boat in action, with plan of the boat*
? early '70's
Pencil, $12\frac{1}{4}$ x $13\frac{1}{8}$ in / 31.1 x 33.3 cm
Derby Museum and Art Gallery

Plate 117   *Sea Battle* ? early '70's
Pencil, $11\frac{1}{2}$ x $13\frac{1}{8}$ in / 29.2 x 33.3 cm
Derby Museum and Art Gallery

Plate 118 *Mrs Coltman* c 1772–73
Charcoal with white heightening on canvas
21⅜ x 17½ in / 54.3 x 43.8 cm
Charles Rogers–Coltman   Cat 43

Plate 119 *Thomas Coltman* c 1772–73
Charcoal with white heightening on canvas
21⅜ x 17½ in / 54.3 x 43.8 cm
Charles Rogers–Coltman   Cat 42

Plate 121 *Young Man in fur cap*
c 1772–73
Chalk c 16 x 12 in / 40.6 x 30.5 cm
J. B. Speed Art Museum, Louisville
Cat 155

Plate 120 *Self-portrait* c 1773
28 x 24 in / 71.1 x 60.9 cm
Mrs Beryl E. Cade   Cat 169

Plate 122 *Head of Old Man* c 1770–73
10⅜ x 8⅝ in / 26.3 x 21.9 cm
Sir Gilbert Inglefield   Cat 187

Plate 123 *The Old Man and Death* 1773
40 x 50 in / 101.7 x 127 cm
Wadsworth Atheneum, Hartford, Conn   Cat 220

Plate 124   *Study of an antique bust, in two
positions* c 1774–75
Oil on paper on canvas 20 x 16½ in / 50.8 x 41.9 cm
Charles E. Buckley   Cat 180

Plate 125   *Study after a Roman portrait
bust* c 1774–75
Brown ink and wash on light blue
paper
14 x 11¾ in / 35.5 x 29.8 cm
Derby Museum and Art Gallery

Plate 126   Drawing after *The Drunken Old Woman*
From Wright's sketchbook 1774
British Museum

Plate 128   Drawing after the *Huntsman and Dog* 1775
Pen on light green paper
$22\frac{3}{8}$ x $13\frac{3}{8}$ in / 56.8 x 33.9 cm
Derby Museum and Art Gallery

Plate 127   Drawing after *The Dying Gaul* 1774
Pencil $13\frac{1}{4}$ x $12\frac{5}{8}$ in / 33.6 x 32 cm
Derby Museum and Art Gallery

Plate 129   Drawing after *Ganymede with
the Eagle* 1774
Pencil 21 x $11\frac{3}{4}$ in / 53.3 x 29.8 cm
Derby Museum and Art Gallery

Plate 130   Drawing after the *Barberini Fawn* 1775
Pen 20½ x 13⅞ in / 52 x 35.2 cm
Derby Museum and Art Gallery

Plate 132   Drawing after the *Panther* and
Ganymede 1774
Pencil 21½ x 14½ in / 54.6 x 36.8 cm
Derby Museum and Art Gallery

Plate 131   Drawing after the *Barberini Fawn* 1775
Pen 20 x 14¼ in / 50.8 x 36.1 cm
Derby Museum and Art Gallery

Plate 133   Drawing after *Satyr* 1774
Pencil 20⅝ x 12¾ in / 52.4 x 32.4 cm
Derby Museum and Art Gallery

Plate 134   *Boy asleep*
From Wright's sketchbook 1774
British Museum

Plate 136   *Man in profile* sketched twice c 1774
Pencil 9 x 7⅜ in / 22.8 x 18.7 cm
Derby Museum and Art Gallery

Plate 135   Drawing after *The Wrestlers* 1774
Pencil 15½ x 14 in / 39.3 x 35.5 cm
Derby Museum and Art Gallery

Plate 137   *Boy with leg up*
From Wright's sketchbook 1774
British Museum

Plate 138   *Boys reclining* 1774
Pencil and brown ink
14¼ x 21⅛ in / 36.2 x 53.6 cm
Derby Museum and Art Gallery

Plate 140   Drawing after *Ecorché* figure
From Wright's sketchbook 1774
British Museum

Plate 139   *Boys reclining*
From Wright's sketchbook 1774
British Museum

Plate 141   *Youth asleep with stick*
From Wright's sketchbook 1774
British Museum

Plate 142   *Villa behind wall* c 1774
Pencil 7 x 7¾ (10¼) / 17.7 x 19.6 (26) cm
Derby Museum and Art Gallery

Plate 143   *Nice landscape* 1773
Grey wash 9¾ x 12¼ in / 24.7 x 31.1 cm
Derby Museum and Art Gallery

Plate 144   Study of a *Man seated* c 1774
Pen and sepia wash 27 x 19 in / 68.6 x 48.3 cm
Derby Museum and Art Gallery

Plate 145   *Part of the Colosseum* c 1774–75
Grey wash 15 x 21½ in / 38.1 x 54.6 cm
Henry E. Huntington Library and Art Gallery

Plate 147   *House built on top of wall* c 1774–75
Watercolour 10⅝ x 16¾ in / 26.9 x 41.6 cm
Derby Museum and Art Gallery

Plate 146   *Part of the Colosseum* c 1774–75
Brown ink and wash
15 x 21¾ in / 38.1 x 54.3 cm
Derby Museum and Art Gallery

Plate 148   *Tree study, Rome* 1774
Pencil on green prepared paper (reverse white)
14¼ x 21⅛ in / 36.2 x 53.6 cm
Derby Museum and Art Gallery

ate 149   *Roman Ruins* c 1774–75
rey wash
ght size 18½ x 12½ in / 46.9 x 31.7 cm
erby Museum and Art Gallery

ate 151   *Ionic Temple, Rome* c 1774–75
ncil and sepia wash
¾ x 12⅝ in / 47.6 x 32 cm
erby Museum and Art Gallery

Plate 150   *Roman Ruins* c 1774–75
Brown ink and wash
11¼ x 9 in / 28.5 x 22.8 cm
Derby Museum and Art Gallery

Plate 152   A letter from the Artist, with a view of Castel
Sant'Angelo and St. Peter's
Pen & wash   9 x 12 in / 22.9 x 30.5 cm
Derby Museum and Art Gallery

Plate 153   Reverse of letter in Plate 152
Derby Museum and Art Gallery

Plate 154   *Girandola from the Castel Sant'Angelo* 1774
Sepia wash with brown ink
Sight size 13¼ x 19¾ in / 33.6 x 50.1 cm
Derby Museum and Art Gallery

Plate 155   Schematic drawing of *St. Peter's* c 1774–75
Brown ink 10⅝ x 17½ in / 29.5 x 44.4 cm
Derby Museum and Art Gallery

Plate 156   *Girandola from the Castel Sant' Angelo* c 1774–75
Watercolour 19 x 12½ in / 48.2 x 31.7 cm
Derby Museum and Art Gallery

Plate 157   *Girandola from the Castel Sant' Angelo* c 1774–75
Pen 14⅝ x 18⅞ in / 37.1 x 47.9 cm
Derby Museum and Art Gallery

96

Plate 158   *View through archway, Rome* c 1774–75
Grey wash sight size 20½ x 13⅝ in / 52 x 34.6 cm
Derby Museum and Art Gallery

Plate 159   *Fire in Rome* 1774
Pen and bistre wash on toned yellow paper
sight size 11 x 16½ in / 27.9 x 41.9 cm
Derby Museum and Art Gallery

Plate 160   *Old man, full face* c 1774–75
Oil on paper pasted on board
c 19 x 14 in / 48.2 x 35.5 cm
Private Collection U.K.   Cat 185

Plate 161   *Old man, profile* c 1774–75
Oil on paper pasted on board
19 x 12 in / 48.2 x 35.5 cm
Private collection U.K.   Cat 186

Plate 162   *The Captive, from Sterne* c 1775–77
40 x 50 in / 101.6 x 127 cm
Derby Museum and Art Gallery   Cat 217

Plate 163   *Eruption of Vesuvius* 1774
Gouache $12\frac{3}{4}$ x $18\frac{3}{8}$ in / 32.4 x 46.7 cm
Derby Museum and Art Gallery

Plate 164   *Vesuvius* 1774
Pencil 12¼ x 17¾ in / 31.1 x 45 cm
Derby Museum and Art Gallery

Plate 165   *Vesuvius* 1774
Pencil 12½ x 16½ in / 31.1 x 41.9 cm
Sir Gilbert Inglefield

Plate 166   *Firework Display at the Castel Sant' Angelo* c 1774–75
16¾ x 28 in / 42.5 x 71.1 cm
Birmingham Art Gallery   Cat 249

Plate 167   *Vesuvius* c 1774–75
16¾ x 28 in / 42.5 x 71.1 cm
L. B. Sanderson   Cat 273

Plate 168   *Vesuvius* c 1774–75
47½ x 67 in / 120.6 x 170.2 cm
Derby Museum and Art Gallery   Cat 275

Plate 169   *Vesuvius in Eruption ?* c 1775–77
40 x 50 in / 101.6 x 127 cm
University College of Wales, Aberystwyth   Cat 274

Plate 170   *Vesuvius in Eruption* mid to late '70's
49 x 71 in / 124.4 x 180.3 cm
Miss D. M. R. Cade   Cat 266

Plate 171   *Grotto in the Gulf of Salerno* 1774
Black chalk 11¼ x 18½ in / 28.5 x 46.9 cm
Private collection U.K.   see Cat 279

Plate 172   *Grotto in the Gulf of Salerno* 1774
Black chalk 11¼ x 18½ in / 28.5 x 46.9 cm
Private collection U.K.   see Cat 280

Plate 173 *Grotto with Waterfall* c 1775–79
15¼ x 19½ in / 38.7 x 49.5 cm
Ian Appleby   Cat 293

Plate 174 *A Cavern, Evening* 1774
40 x 50 in / 101.6 x 127 cm
Smith College Museum of Art   Cat 282

Plate 175 *A Cavern, Morning* 1774
40 x 50 in / 101.6 x 127 cm
Mr and Mrs R. Kirk Askew Jr   Cat 281

Plate 176   *William Alvey Darwin* 1776
30 x 25 in / 76.2 x 63.5 cm
Mrs Richard Kindersley   Cat 55

Plate 177   *Jane Darwin and her son William Brown Darwin* 1776
30 x 25 in / 76.2 x 63.5 cm
Mrs Richard Kindersley   Cat 56

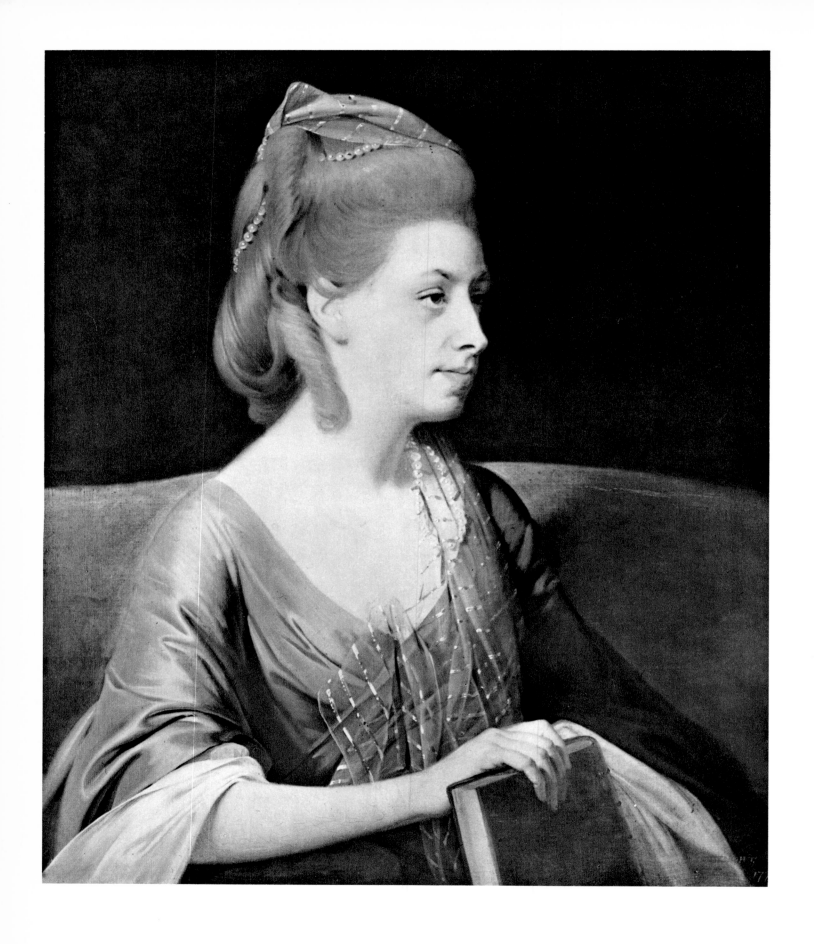

Plate 178   *Mrs Edward Witts* 1776
30 x 25 in / 76.2 x 63.5 cm
Major General F. V. B. Witts   Cat 150

Plate 179   *Edwin, from Dr Beattie's Minstrel* c 1777–78
63 x 46 in / 160 x 116.8 cm
Lady Cynthia Colville   Cat 235

Plate 180   *Charles Stead Hope as a boy* c 1776–77
Oval 13½ x 11½ in / 34.3 x 29.2 cm
Private collection U.K.   Cat 89

Plate 181   *Miss Harriet Hope* c 1776–77
Oval 14 x 12 in / 35.5 x 30.5 cm
H. R. Edwards   Cat 90

Plate 182   *William Hayley* 1776
Grisaille oval 13¼ x 11½ in / 34.3 x 29.2 cm
Private collection U.K.   Cat 75

Plate 183   *Mrs William Hayley* 1776
Grisaille oval 13¼ x 11½ in / 34.3 x 29.2 cm
Private collection U.K.   Cat 76

Plate 184   *Maria and her dog Sylvio* 1777
32½ x 49½ in / 82.5 x 125.7 cm
Private collection U.K.   Cat 236

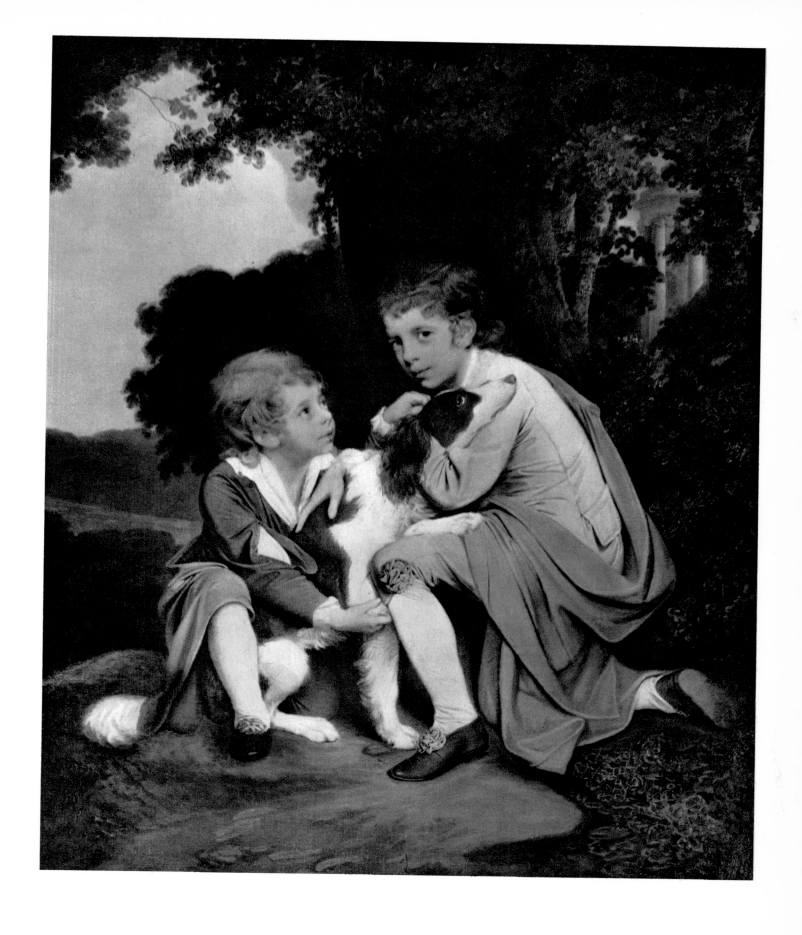

Plate 185   *Pickford Children* c 1777
58 x 48 in / 147.3 x 121.9 cm
Private collection U.K.   Cat 119

Plate 186   'H. B.' Hall c 1776–78
30 x 25 in / 76.2 x 63.5 cm
Hugh Wontner M. V. O., J. P.   Cat 72

Plate 187   Mrs Hall c 1776–78
30 x 25 in / 76.2 x 63.5 cm
Mrs Nancie C. MacGilp   Cat 73

Plate 188 'Elizabeth Kennion, Mrs Smyth' c 1776–78
30 x 25 in / 76.2 x 63.5 cm
W. R. Kennion   Cat 131

Plate 189   Mrs Hodges c 1775–76
30 x 25 in / 76.2 x 63.5 cm
Formerly Humphrey Roberts collection
Cat 83

117

Plate 190   *Richard Cheslyn* 1777
50 x 40 in / 127 x 101.6 cm
Private collection U.K.   Cat 38

Plate 191   *Thomas Gisborne* 1777
30 x 25 in / 76.2 x 63.5 cm
Mr and Mrs Patrick Gibson   Cat 66

Plate 192   *Mrs Beridge* 1777
50 x 40 in / 127 x 101.6 cm
Minneapolis Institute of Arts   Cat 18

119

Plate 193   *Robert Holden* c 1778–79
50 x 40 in / 127 x 101.6 cm
Major H. R. Holden   Cat 84

Plate 194   *John Whetham of Kirklington* c 1778–79
50 x 40 in / 127 x 101.6 cm
Major H. R. Holden   Cat 140

Plate 195   *John Whetham of Kirklington* c 1778–79
50 x 40 in / 127 x 101.6 cm
Mrs Daphne M. Smith   Cat 139

Plate 196   'Henry Flint' c 1778–80
30 x 25 in / 76.2 x 63.5 cm
D. R. Sherborn   Cat 61

Plate 198   Henry Richmond c 1777–80
30 x 25 in / 76.2 x 63.5 cm
Professor Oliffe Richmond   Cat 125

Plate 197   Rev William (?) Pickering c 1777–80
30 x 25 in / 76.2 x 63.5 cm
Sir Gilbert Inglefield   Cat 118

Plate 199   'John Harrison' 1779–80
30 x 25 in / 76.2 x 63.5 cm
Private collection U.K.   Cat 74

Plate 200   'Hon Thomas Bligh' c 1777–80
30 x 25 in / 76.2 x 63.5 cm
Manchester City Art Galleries   Cat 19

Plate 201   Charles Roe c 1777–80
30 x 25 in / 76.2 x 63.5 cm
Parish of Christ Church, Macclesfield   Cat 126

Plate 202   Lynford Caryl   c 1780
30 x 25 in / 76.2 x 63.5 cm
Jesus College, Cambridge   Cat 33

Plate 203   *Mrs Francis Hurt* c 1780
50 x 40 in / 127 x 101.6 cm
Michael Hurt   Cat 93

Plate 204   *Francis Hurt of Alderwasley* c 1780
50 x 40 in / 127 x 101.6 cm
Michael Hurt   Cat 92

Plate 205 *William Chase* c 1779–81
30 x 25 in / 76.2 x 63.5 cm
Yale University Art Gallery (gift of Junius S. & Henry S. Morgan)
Cat 35

Plate 206   *Samuel Crompton* c 1780
30 x 25 in / 76.2 x 63.5 cm
Colonel Sir John Crompton-Inglefield   Cat 46

Plate 207   *Mrs Samuel Crompton* c 1780
30 x 25 in / 76.2 x 63.5 cm
Colonel Sir John Crompton-Inglefield   Cat 47

Plate 208   *Robert Bakewell* c 1780
50 x 40 in / 127 x 101.6 cm
Richard Dyott   Cat 11

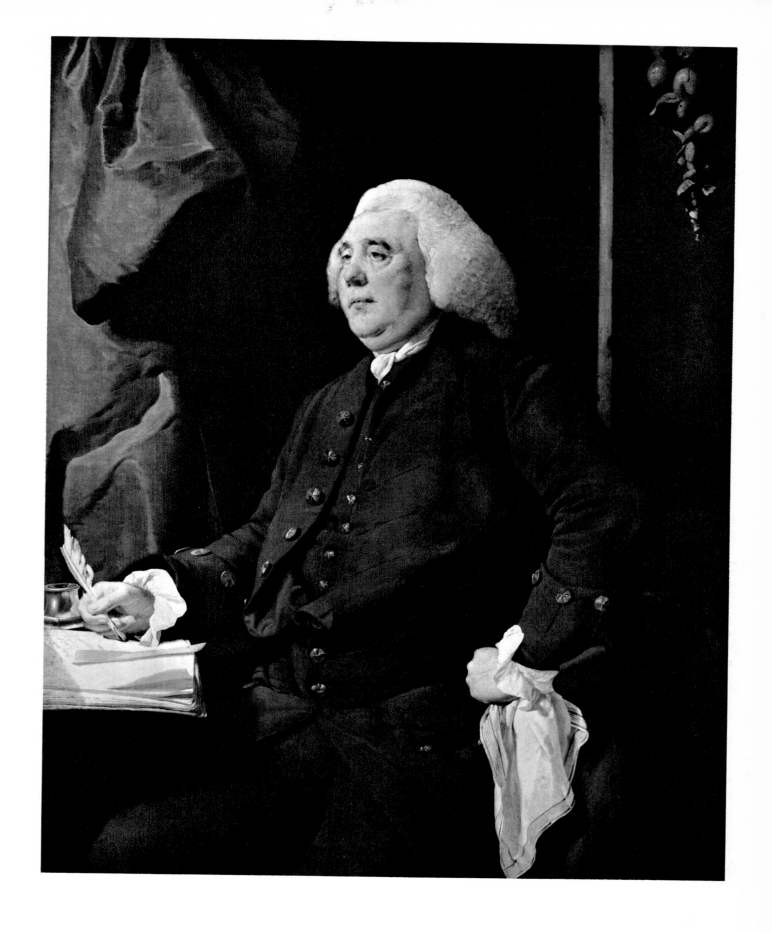

Plate 209 *'Christopher Heath'* c 1781
50 x 40 in / 127 x 101.6 cm
Private collection U.K.   Cat 78

Plate 210   *Firework Display at the Castel Sant'Angelo* c 1775–78
55¼ x 68⅛ in / 140.3 x 173 cm
Walker Art Gallery, Liverpool   Cat 250

Plate 211   *A Grotto in the Kingdom of Naples with Banditti:*
A Sunset c 1777–78
48 x 68 in / 121.9 x 172.7 cm
G. Meynell M.B.E.   Cat 277

Plate 212   *Matlock High Tor, moonlight* c 1777–79
24 x 29 in / 60.9 x 73.6 cm
Leicester Museum and Art Gallery   Cat 307

Plate 213   *Firework Display at the Castel Sant'Angelo* 1778–79
63¾ x 84 in / 161.9 x 213.3 cm
Hermitage Museum, Leningrad   Cat 251

Plate 214   *Vesuvius with the procession of St Januerius' Head* 1778
63¾ x 84 in / 161.9 x 213.3 cm
Pushkin Museum, Moscow   Cat 268

Plate 215   *Grotto with the figure of Julia* 1780
c 48 x 67 in / 121.9 x 172.7 cm
G. Meynell M.B.E.   Cat 278

Plate 216   *Grotto with the figure of Julia* 1780
15½ x 20 in / 39.4 x 50.8 cm
R. D. Plant   Cat 283

134

Plate 217   *Matlock Tor, Moonlight ?* c 1778–80
25 x 30 in / 63.5 x 76.2 cm
Mr and Mrs Paul Mellon   Cat 308

Plate 218   *Matlock Tor, Moonlight* c 1778–80
25 x 30 in / 63.5 x 76.2 cm
Detroit Institute of Arts   Cat 309

Plates 219, 219a *Brooke Boothby* 1780–81
58¼ x 81¼ in / 148 x 206.4 cm
Tate Gallery   Cat 20

Plate 220   *Maria, from Sterne* 1781
63 x 45½ in / 160 x 115.6 cm
Derby Museum and Art Gallery   Cat 237

Plate 221 *Synnot Children* c 1780–81
60 x 49½ in / 152.4 x 125.8 cm
Mrs Michael Hawker, S. Australia   Cat 135

Plate 222   *Two Young Gentlemen in the character of Archers*
c 1781–82
71½ x 54 in / 181.6 x 137.2 cm
Oscar & Peter Johnson Ltd.   Cat 111

Plate 223 *Rev. Henry Case (afterwards Case-Morewood)* 1782
50 x 40 in / 127 x 101.6 cm
Palmer-Morewood Collection: on loan to Brighton Art
Gallery   Cat 108

Plate 224   *Helen Morewood* 1782
50 x 40 in / 127 x 101.6 cm
Palmer-Morewood Collection: on loan to Brighton Art
Gallery   Cat 109

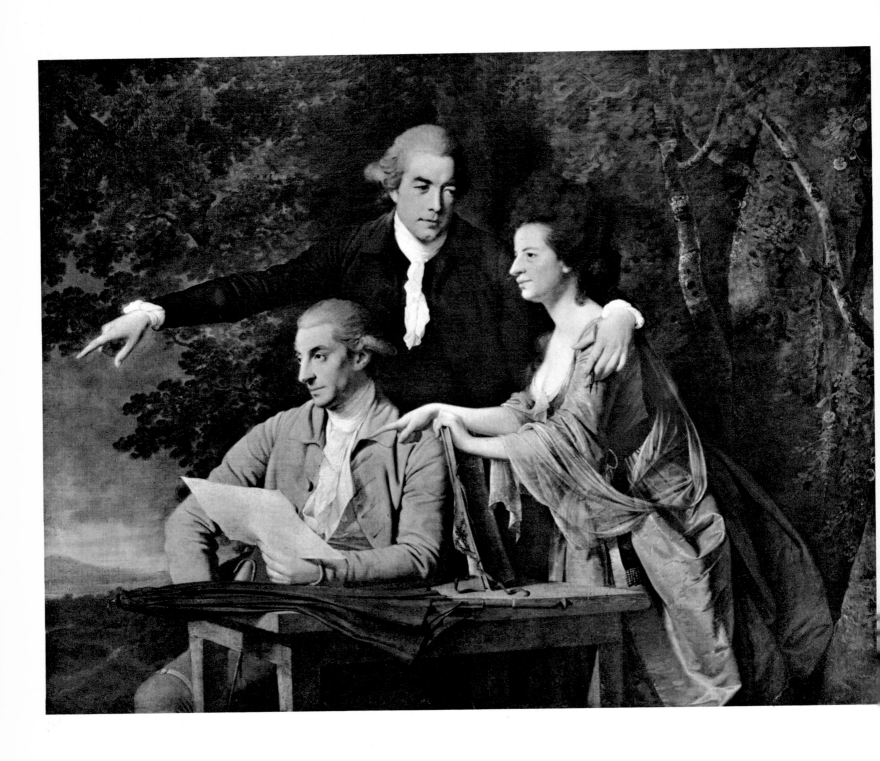

Plate 225   *Rev d'Ewes Coke, his wife Hannah and Daniel Parker Coke, M.P.* c 1780–82
60 x 70 in / 152.4 x 177.8 cm
Derby Museum and Art Gallery   Cat 40

Plate 226   *A Philosopher by Lamplight* c 1778–81
50 x 40 in / 127 x 101.6 cm
Private collection U.K.   Cat 194

Plate 227   *John Whitehurst, F.R.S.* c 1782–83
$36\frac{1}{4}$ x 28 in / 92.1 x 71.1 cm
John Smith & Sons, Derby   Cat 141

Plate 228   *Head of Old Man* c 1780–81
36⅛ x 27⅞ in / 91.7 x 70.8 cm
Mrs Edward Maclean Stewart   Cat 181

Plate 229 *Samuel Ward* c 1782–83 or later
30 x 25 in / 76.2 x 63.5 cm
Derby Museum and Art Gallery   Cat 137

Plate 230 *Rev. Thomas Seward* c 1782–83
30 x 25 in / 76.2 x 63.5 cm
Untraced   Cat 128

Plate 231   *Virgil's Tomb* 1782
40 x 50 in / 101.6 x 127 cm
Private collection U.K.   Cat 288

Plate 232   *Virgil's Tomb* 1779
40 x 50 in / 101.6 x 127 cm
Colonel Sir John Crompton-Inglefield   Cat 287

Plate 233   *Vesuvius* ? early '80's
12 x 14 in / 30.5 x 33.5 cm
Private collection U.K.   Cat 270

Plate 234   *Lake of Nemi* 1782
12 x 14 in / 30.5 x 33.5 cm
Private collection U.K.   Cat 254

Plate 235   *Classical Villa by sea shore* 1782
12 x 14 in / 30.5 x 33.5 cm
Private collection U.K.   Cat 255

Plate 236   *Landscape with ruins, by moonlight*
? c 1780–82
25 x 30 in / 63.5 x 76.2 cm
Miss D. M. R. Cade   Cat 305

Plate 237   *Lake of Nemi, Sunset* c 1780–82
24¼ x 29¾ in / 61.6 x 75.5 cm
Private collection U.K.   Cat 252

Plate 238   Study for Plate 237 c 1780–81
Black chalk with white heightening and wash
on light green paper
7¼ x 9 in / 18.4 x 22.8 cm
Derby Museum and Art Gallery

Plate 239   *Lake by Moonlight* c 1780–82
4¼ x 29¾ in / 61.6 x 75.5 cm
Mr and Mrs Paul Mellon   Cat 253

Plate 240   Study for Plate 239 ? c 1780–81
Pen and wash with white heightening on light
green paper
7¼ x 9 in / 18.4 x 22.8 cm
Derby Museum and Art Gallery

Plate 241   *William and Margaret* c 1784–85
48 x 56 in / 121.9 x 142.2 cm
Colonel Sir John Crompton-Inglefield:
on loan to Judges' Lodgings, Derby   Cat 226

Plate 242   *Penelope unravelling her Web* 1783–84
40 x 50 in / 101.6 x 127 cm
Mr and Mrs Hensleigh Wedgwood   Cat 225

Plate 243   *Leaper Children* c 1785
68 x 54 in / 172.7 x 137.2 cm
Private collection U.K.   Cat 100

Plate 244   *Arkwright's Cotton Mills, by night* c 1782–83
34 x 45 in / 86.3 x 114.3 cm
I. M. Booth   Cat 311

Plate 245   *The Corinthian Maid* c 1783–84
42 x 50 in / 106.7 x 127 cm
Mr and Mrs Paul Mellon   Cat 224

Plate 246   *The Lady in Milton's 'Comus'* 1784
40½ x 50¾ in / 102.8 x 128.9 cm
Walker Art Gallery, Liverpool   Cat 234

Plate 247   *The Indian Widow* 1783–85
40 x 50 in / 101.6 x 127 cm
Derby Museum and Art Gallery   Cat 243

Plate 248 *Matlock Tor, daylight* mid-'80's
28½ x 38½ in / 72.4 x 97.8 cm
Fitzwilliam Museum, Cambridge Cat 310

Plate 249   *Landscape with Dale Abbey* c 1785
28½ x 39 in / 72.4 x 99 cm
Sheffield City Art Galleries   Cat 331

Plate 250   *Bridge with Turret over Winding River* 1785
30 x 38 in / 76.2 x 96.5 cm
Royal Borough of Kensington and Chelsea Public Libraries
(Leighton House)   Cat 291

Plate 251   *Cascade at Tivoli* ? c 1786
Pencil and watercolour, sight size $14\frac{1}{2}$ x $20\frac{1}{4}$ in / 36.8 x 51.4 cm
Derby Museum and Art Gallery

Plate 252   'Dovedale' 1786
25 x 33 in / 63.5 x 83.8 cm
Mrs George Anson   Cat 319

Plate 253   Study for Plate 252 c 1786
Wash 14¼ x 21 in / 36 x 53 cm
Derby Museum and Art Gallery.

Plate 254 'Dovedale' ? early to mid-'80's
Watercolour 17 x 10 in / 43.2 x 25.4 cm
Derby Museum and Art Gallery

Plate 255 View in Dovedale 1786
18 x 25 in / 45.7 x 63.5 cm
Viscount Scarsdale Cat 315

Plate 256   *The Colosseum, daylight* ? mid–'80's
41 x 51 in / 104 x 129 cm
Derby Museum and Art Gallery   Cat 246

Plate 257   *Convent of S. Cosimato* 1786
18 x 25 in / 45.7 x 63.5 cm
Viscount Scarsdale   Cat 262

Plate 258   *Dovedale in Sunlight* c 1784–88
25 x 31 in / 63.5 x 78.7 cm
Colonel Sir John Crompton-Inglefield   Cat 316

Plate 259   *View of the Boathouse near Matlock*
? mid-'80's
23 x 30 in / 58.5 x 76 cm
Mr and Mrs Paul Mellon   Cat 303

Plate 260   *View of Tivoli* ? c 1783–86
30 x 38 in / 76.2 x 96.5 cm
Derby Museum and Art Gallery   Cat 265

Plate 261   *Dovedale by Moonlight* c 1784–88
25 x 31 in / 63.5 x 78.7 cm
Allen Memorial Museum, Oberlin College
Cat 317

Plate 262 *Lake with Castle on a Hill* 1787
Diameter 24 in / 60.9 cm
Gooden & Fox Ltd   Cat 330

Plate 263   *River in a Rocky Gorge* 1787
11½ x 17 in / 29.2 x 43.2 cm
Private collection U.K.   Cat 327

Plate 264   *Dovedale, morning* c 1787–90
20 x 29 in / 50.8 x 73.6 cm
H. R. Edwards   Cat 318

Plate 265   *Chee Tor* ? late '80's
17 x 23 in / 43.1 x 58.4 cm
Colonel Sir John Crompton-Inglefield   Cat 302

Plate 266   *Dorothy Gell of Hopton* 1786
93½ x 57 in / 236.8 x 144.8 cm
Lieut Colonel John Chandos-Pole O.B.E.   Cat 65

Plate 267   *Rev Basil Bury Beridge* c 1785
50 x 40 in / 127 x 101.6 cm
Kunsthistorisches Museum, Vienna   Cat 17

Plate 268   'Stephen' Jones 1785
50 x 40 in / 127 x 101.6 cm
Sir Gilbert Inglefield   Cat 97

Plate 269   *The Rev and Mrs Thomas Gisborne* 1786
74 x 60 in / 188 x 152.4 cm
Mr and Mrs Paul Mellon   Cat 67

Plate 271   '*Dr Richard Wright*'
c 1785–87
30 x 25 in / 76.2 x 63.5 cm
Mr and Mrs Paul Mellon   Cat 173

Plate 270   *Thomas Pares* c 1785–88
50 x 40 in / 127 x 101.6 cm
Major J. Pares   Cat 116

Plate 273   *Richard Wright* c 1786–88
30 x 25 in / 76.2 x 63.5 cm
Private Collection U.K.   Cat 179

Plate 272   Copy after Joseph Wright *Captain Salmon* c 1787–88
30 x 25 in / 76.2 x 63.5 cm
Private Collection U.K.   See page 218

Plate 274   *Mrs Holland of Ford* c 1787
30 x 25 in / 76.2 x 63.5 cm
Gladwyn Turbutt   Cat 86

Plate 275   *John Holland of Ford* 1787
30 x 25 in / 76.2 x 63.5 cm
Gladwyn Turbutt   Cat 85

Plate 276   *Sarah Wood* c 1789
30 x 25 in / 76.2 x 63.5 cm
Private Collection U.K.   Cat 153

Plate 277   *Hugh Wood* c 1789
30 x 25 in / 76.2 x 63.5 cm
Private Collection U.K.   Cat 152

Plate 278 *Thornhill Children* c 1789–90
57 x 48½ in / 144.8 x 123.2 cm
Private Collection U.K. Cat 136

Plate 279 *Wood Children* 1789
66 x 53 in / 167.7 x 134.7 cm
Derby Museum and Art Gallery   Cat 151

Plate 280   *Lady Wilmot and her Child* 1788
c 79 x 66 in / 200 x 167.7 cm
Mrs George Anson   Cat 149

Plate 281   *The Dead Soldier* 1789
40 x 50 in / 101.6 x 127 cm
James Ricau   Cat 240

Plate 282   *Convent of S. Cosimato* c 1787–90
19⅞ x 25 in / 50.5 x 63.5 cm
Walker Art Gallery, Liverpool   Cat 264

Plate 283   *Convent of S. Cosimato* 1789
24 x 32 in / 60.9 x 81.3 cm
J. T. Blundell–Turner on loan to Derby Museum and Art
Gallery   Cat 263

Plate 284 *Small Prison Scene* c 1787–90
15½ x 18½ in / 39.4 x 47 cm
Mr and Mrs Paul Mellon   Cat 218

Plate 286 *Interior of a prison*
Grey wash with brown ink, touches of pencil under drawing
13 x 17½ in / 33 x 44.4 cm
H. Cornish Torbock

Plate 285 *Small Prison scene*
19 x 27 in / 48.2 x 68.5 cm
Private Collection U.K.   Cat 219

Plate 287   *Sunset on the Coast near Naples* ? mid to late '80's
25 x 29⅞ in / 63.5 x 75.9 cm
Sir Gilbert Inglefield   Cat 284

Plate 288   *Vesuvius from Posillipo* ? late '80's
Copper 7½ x 9 in / 19 x 22.8 cm
Christopher Norris   Cat 271

Plate 289   *Vesuvius in eruption* ? late '80's
Copper, 7½ x 9 in / 19. x 22.8 cm
Christopher Norris   Cat 272

Plate 290   *View near Matlock by moonlight*
? c 1788–90
15 x 23⅛ in / 38.1 x 58.7 cm
Colonel Sir John Crompton-Inglefield;
on loan to the Judges' Lodgings, Derby
Cat 306

Plate 291   *Vesuvius from Posillipo* 178(9?)
40½ x 50½ in / 102.8 x 128.2 cm
Major Peter Miller Mundy   Cat 267

Plate 292   *Lake by Moonlight with Castle on Hill* 178(8?)
22⅞ x 30 in / 58 x 76.2 cm
Palmer-Morewood Collection;
on loan to Brighton Art Gallery   Cat 333

Plate 293   *Cottage on Fire* c 1787–88
22⅞ x 30 in / 58 x 76.2 cm
Palmer-Morewood Collection;
on loan to Brighton Art Gallery   Cat 334

Plate 294   *Vesuvius from Posillipo* c 1788
Panel 25 x 33 in / 63.5 x 83.8 cm
Mrs George Anson   Cat 269

Plate 295 *Classical Villa by sea shore ?* c 1787–90
21 x 36 in / 53.3 x 91.4 cm
Mrs V. Martin   Cat 294

Plate 296   *Ruined Archway* ? 1790
24½ x 17½ in / 62.2 x 44.4 cm
Private Collection U.S.A.   Cat 297

Plate 297   *View near Cromford* 1789
Pencil and watercolour 16⅝ x 13 in /
42.2 x 33 cm
Derby Museum and Art Gallery

The seat of ye figures

perhaps the Neech wt. contain the Sarcophagus iĩ. be better removed a little more to the right wt. wd. give a greater breadth of illuminated wall —

Plate 298　Drawing for *Romeo and Juliet* c 1787–88
Pencil 7¼ x 8¾ in / 18.4 x 22.2 cm
Derby Museum and Art Gallery

Plate 299　Engraving by Robert Thew after
Joseph Wright (1800)
Ferdinand and Miranda in Prospero's Cell
Original painting 102 x 144 in / 259 x 365.8 cm
Cat 233

189

Plate 300 *Charles Hurt of Wirksworth* c 1788
$90\frac{1}{2}$ x $54\frac{1}{2}$ in / 229.9 x 138.5 cm
Formerly Hurt Collection   Cat 94

Plate 301   Mezzotint (1911) after an
untraced Wright
Susannah, wife of Charles Hurt and daughter of Sir
Richard Arkwright c 1788   See Cat 95

Plate 302   Engraving by S. Middiman (1794) after
Joseph Wright
Antigonus in the Storm, from The Winter's Tale
Original painting c 70 x 95 in /
177.8 x 241.3 cm   Cat 230

Plate 303   *Cottage on Fire* c 1790
25 x 30 in / 63.5 x 76.2 cm
Derby Museum and Art Gallery   Cat 336

Plate 304   *Antigonus in the Storm, from The Winter's Tale* 1790
61 x 85 in / 154.9 x 215.9 cm
Viscount Scarsdale   Cat 231

Plate 305   *Romeo and Juliet* c 1787–91
70 x 95 in / 177.8 x 241.3 cm
J. M. Oakes   Cat 232

Plate 306 *Cottage on Fire* c 1790
22¼ x 31½ in / 56.5 x 80 cm
Mr and Mrs Paul Mellon   Cat 338

Plate 307 *Cottage on Fire* c 1790
22¾ x 29½ in / 57.8 x 74.3 cm
Mr and Mrs David Giles Carter   Cat 337

Plate 308 *River Valley (? Derbyshire)*
11¾ x 17¾ in / 29.8 x 45 cm
Dr and Mrs William S. Dale   Cat 300

Plate 309 *Landscape with Figures and Waggon* c 1790
40 x 50 in / 101.6 x 127 cm
Southampton Art Gallery   Cat 299

Plate 310   *Lake Scene* 1790
21½ x 30 in / 54.6 x 76.2 cm
Mr and Mrs Michael D. Coe   Cat 301

Plate 311   *Italian Landscape* 1790
40½ x 51 in / 102.8 x 129.5 cm
Mr and Mrs Paul Mellon   Cat 292

Plate 312   *Lighthouse in the Mediterranean* early '90's
14¼ x 20 in / 36.2 x 50.8 cm
K. J. Blunt, on loan to Derby Museum and Art Gallery   Cat 295

Plate 313   *Lighthouse on the Coast of Tuscany* ? 1789
40 x 50½ in / 101.6 x 128.2 cm
Tate Gallery   Cat 296

Plate 314   *Albano ? c 1790–92*
17½ x 25 in / 44.4 x 63.5 cm
Major J. W. Chandos-Pole   Cat 259

Plate 315   *Albano c 1790*
39¼ x 48 in / 99.7 x 121.9 cm
National Museum of Wales   Cat 260

Plate 316   *Albano* c 1790–92
$14\frac{1}{4}$ x $21\frac{1}{2}$ in / 36.2 x 54.6 cm
Mr and Mrs Paul Mellon   Cat 257

Plate 317   *Nemi* c 1790–92
$14\frac{1}{4}$ x $21\frac{1}{2}$ in / 36.2 x 54.6 cm
Mr and Mrs Paul Mellon   Cat 258

Plate 318   *Nemi*
17 x 24 in / 43.2 x 60.9 cm
Dr and Mrs William S. Dale   Cat 256

Plate 319   *Nemi*
17¾ x 25½ in / 45 x 64.7 cm
Private Collection U.K.   Cat 261

Plate 320 *Boy blowing Bladder* 1790
30 x 25 in / 76.2 x 63.5 cm
Colonel Peter Arkwright Cat 210

Plate 321 *Girl looking through Bladder* c 1790
30 x 25 in / 76.2 x 63.5 cm
Colonel Peter Arkwright Cat 211

Plate 322 *Harriet Wright (daughter of the artist)*
c 1790
Panel 10 x 8⅜ in / 25.4 x 21.3 cm
Derby Museum and Art Gallery Cat 178

Plate 323   *Sir Richard Arkwright* 1789–90
95 x 60 in / 241.3 x 152.4 cm
Colonel Peter Arkwright   Cat 1

Plate 324   *Jedediah Strutt* c 1790
50 x 40 in / 127 x 101.6 cm
The Lord Belper   Cat 133

Plate 325   *Richard Arkwright, his wife Mary and Child* 1790
96 x 62½ in / 243.8 x 158.7 cm
Colonel Peter Arkwright   Cat 3

Plate 326 *Bridge through a Cavern, Moonlight* 1791
25 x 32 in / 63.5 x 81.2 cm
Derby Museum and Art Gallery Cat 276

Plate 327 *Distant view of Florence* c 1789–93
22½ x 29½ in / 57.1 x 74.9 cm
Art Institute of Chicago Cat 290

Plate 328   *Three Children of Richard Arkwright with a Goat* 1791
77 x 60 in / 195.6 x 152.4 cm
Colonel Peter Arkwright   Cat 4

Plate 329   *Three Children of Richard Arkwright with a Kite* 1791
77 x 60 in / 195.6 x 152.4 cm
Colonel Peter Arkwright   Cat 5

Plate 330   *Willersley Castle, Cromford* c 1790
23 x 30 in / 58.4 x 76.2 cm
Formerly Col M. H. Grant   Cat 313

Plate 331   *Arkwright's Cotton Mills, by day* c 1790
23 x 30 in / 58.4 x 76.2 cm
Formerly Col M. H. Grant   Cat 312

Plate 332   *Fire seen through Trees* 1793
16 x 21½ in / 40.6 x 54.6 cm
Dr and Mrs William S. Dale   Cat 335

Plate 333   *Cut through the Rock, Cromford* c 1790
18⅛ x 22⅛ in / 46 x 56.2 cm
Dr and Mrs William S. Dale   Cat 314

Plate 334   *Thomas Oldknow* c 1790–91
86 x 56½ in / 218.4 x 143.5 cm
D. R. Sherborn F.S.A.   Cat 114

Plate 335   *Samuel Oldknow* c 1790–92
c 85 x 55 in / 215.9 x 139.5 cm
Leeds City Art Gallery   Cat 115

Plate 336   *Richard Sacheverell Bateman as a boy* c 1792–94
50 x 40 in / 127 x 101.6 cm
Mrs F. E. Fitz Herbert Wright   Cat 13

Plate 337   *Miss Sally Duesbury* c 1790–95
50 x 40 in / 127 x 101.6 cm
Untraced (U.S.A.)   Cat 59

Plate 338 *Erasmus Darwin* 1792–93
30 x 25 in / 76.2 x 63.5 cm
Major J. W. Chandos-Pole Cat 52

Plate 339   'Dorothy Hunt, wife of Francis Fox' 1793–97
30 x 25 in / 76.2 x 63.5 cm
Mrs D. Hamilton   Cat 63

Plate 340   'Francis Fox' 1793–97
30 x 25 in / 76.2 x 63.5 cm
Mrs D. Hamilton   Cat 62

Plate 341   *George Buckston* c 1795
30 x 25 in / 76.2 x 63.5 cm
Private Collection U.K.   Cat 26

Plate 342   *Sacheverell Pole* c 1794
30 x 25 in / 76.2 x 63.5 cm
Major J. W. Chandos-Pole   Cat 124

Plate 343   *The Twins – Sarah and Anne Haden* c 1795
21½ x 18½ in / 54.6 x 47 cm
Private Collection U.K.   Cat 70

Plate 344   *Moonlight* 1792
36⅛ x 50 in / 91.7 x 127 cm
The University of Liverpool; loan to the Walker Art Gallery
Cat 342

Plate 345   *View of the Head of Ullswater Lake* c 1794–95
c. 63 x 70 in / 160 x 177.8 cm
Formerly Arkwright collection   Cat 321

Plate 346 *Lake District Landscape* 1794
25 x 48 in / 63.5 x 121.9 cm
Private collection U.K. Cat 326

Plate 347 *Landscape with a Rainbow – 'View near Chesterfield'*
c 1794–95
32 x 42 in / 81.2 x 106.7 cm
Derby Museum and Art Gallery Cat 298

Plate 348   *Quirinal (?) by Moonlight*
10½ x 15½ in / 26.7 x 39.4 cm
Dr and Mrs William S. Dale   Cat 248

Plate 349   *Landscape with Ruined Castle* c 1794–95
12 x 18 in / 30.5 x 45.7 cm
Dr and Mrs William S. Dale   Cat 332